YouTube Strategies:
Making And Marketing
Online Video

Paul Colligan
http://www.21QuestionsAboutYouTube.com
http://www.PaulColligan.com
http://www.InstantCustomer.com
http://www.TrafficGeyser.com

YouTube Strategies: Making And Marketing Online Video

© 2013, Colligan.com, Inc.

Colligan.com, Inc.
16200 SW Pacific Highway
Suite H, PCB 254
Tigard, Oregon 97224
Colligan@Gmail.com

The beauty of self-publishing is that I can say something really snarky here and the legal department won't get all up in my face about it. How cool is that?

I've said it a couple of other places in this book, but I'll say it again here, make sure to register this thing. YouTube will change, and if I don't have your email, I won't be able to let you know.

Dedication

Thank you Heidi, for loving me. It makes it all possible.

Thank you Lindsey and Paige for believing in me.

Thank you Steve, Chad, and Jawed for making something so awesome.

Thank you Julie for that debate (way back when), and for being my YouTube Secret Weapon.

Thank you Mike for bringing automation to the game and for making so many of my tests possible.

Thank you Amy and Haley for eMarketing Vids Season 1.

Thank you to the dozens of you who, at sometime in your career, had to point a camera at me or edit my ramblings. You made me look much better than I deserve.

Thank you to anyone who has watched one of my videos. Extra thanks to those who shared, embedded, etc.

Thank you for reading this. I appreciate your trus

Special Offer

YouTube will change. I want to make sure you are up to date when it does.

Visit the following link:

http://0s4.com/r/YTSB

Or scan this QR code:

I'll make sure to keep you up to date with any major information that changes anything I might have written in this book.

In addition, I have more than 3 hours of YouTube Video Training that I'll give you access to as well.

Table Of Contents

About The Author   3

About This Book   5

Is YouTube Really A Social Network? How   9
Can You Leverage That Fact?

How Do I Make The Best Of The New   14
YouTube Live Options?

How Can I Optimize My YouTube Channel   18
And Videos?

What Can I Do To Maximize My YouTube   23
Channel?

How Should I Integrate My YouTube   29
Strategies With Other Social Networks?

How Do You Get Your YouTube Video   33
Ranked On The Front Page Of Google?

What Are The Best SEO Methods And Strategies For A YouTube Video?   39

What Equipment And Software Do I Need To Create A Decent Quality Video?   45

What Value Is There In Closed Captioning Your YouTube Videos?   50

What Is The Ideal Length For A YouTube Video?   55

How Should I Use YouTube Annotations?   59

How Do I Make My Video Go "Viral?"   66

What Quality Should I Publish My YouTube Videos In?   71

How Do I Get My Videos To Link Outside Of YouTube?   75

What Is The Best Format For A YouTube Video?   81

What Should I Do After I Publish My YouTube Video?   84

When Should I Use YouTube And The YouTube Player? When Should I Not?   90

Is It Better To Have One YouTube Channel   95
For Everything I Do?

When Should I Let YouTube Place Ads On My   100
Videos?

What Are The Best Third Party Tools And   105
Services For YouTube?

Should I Use Services To Get More Views For   110
My YouTube Videos?

Now What?   116

About The Author

Paul Colligan helps others leverage technology to improve themselves and broaden their audience with reduced stress and no dramas. He does this with a lifestyle and business designed to answer the challenges and opportunities of this new economy. If you are looking for titles: Husband, Father, Director of Content Marketing for InstantCustomer.com and CEO of Colligan.com. He lives in Portland, Oregon with his wife and daughters and enjoys theater, music, great food, and travel.

Paul believes in building systems and products that work for the user – not vice versa. With that focus, he has played a key role in the launch of dozens of successful Web and Internet products that have seen tens of millions of visitors and dollars in revenue. Previous projects have included work with Traffic Geyser, Rubicon International, Piranha Marketing, Microsoft, and Pearson Education. In addition, he's helped dozens of authors launch their books to top ten at Amazon and has been the secret weapon behind millions of video views at YouTube. Topics of passion include (but are not limited to): new media content creation, product development, lifestyle design, and community building.

Paul's take on the Internet can be seen/heard/read in Web Shows that include eMarketingVids, books that include the Kindle Bestsellers "Cross Channel Social Media Marketing" and "YouTube Strategies" and publications online and off as varied as the Huffington Post. He is a popular speaker on Internet technology topics and frequently speaks online, on the air, and before audiences about his passions. He has presented at events around the world that include BlogWorld and New Media Expo, The European Business Podcasting Summit, Google Tech Talks, Mac World, Social Media Success Summit, and Microsoft Tech-Ed.

If you are interested in his latest projects and/or thoughts on the industry that has been so good to him, there is plenty more to do, read, watch, and ponder at www.PaulColligan.com.

About This Book

I love YouTube. Always have. Always will. She's been very good to me, not just at my Colligan Channel, but through a number of partners and ventures online. With me and my "face for radio," I'm confident in saying anyone can see success on YouTube with the right strategies.

That's why I wrote this …

I did a few courses about YouTube that sold well, and made some good money, but I always got frustrated with the simple reality that whenever we would put something out there, YouTube would change their interface.

Funny thing is, there are some things about YouTube that will never changed / or at least haven't changed yet. Despite all the interface changes, the whole Google+ integration and everything else, the core of what I've taught stands true.

But, unfortunately, it all stands true against screenshots and videos from interfaces "so last week."

So, with that, I release this book. It's the top 21 questions I get asked about YouTube (as well as a few that people should be asking). At the end of each answer is an even shorter summary and a few action items. Put them to good use.

The screens might change. The interface might get gussied up, but the stuff here, won't change.

Cool thing is, if it does, I'll just update the book. Register (as per a few pages back) and I'll keep you up to date.

Fair enough?

Want 21 (free) videos about YouTube and marketing on YouTube? Take a look at -

http://www.21QuestionsAboutYouTube.com

If you'd like to register your book so I can keep you up to date when we make changes (and, with YouTube, you know it will be often), take a look at -

http://www.YouTubeStrategiesBook.com

Thoughts / comments? I'd love to hear them:
http://PaulColligan.com/YouTube
http://PaulColligan.com/GooglePlus
http://PaulColligan.com/Amazon
http://PaulColligan.com/Twitter
http://PaulColligan.com/Facebook

http://YouTubeStrategiesBook.com

Paul Colligan
Portland, Oregon
YouTube Strategies 1.2
April 2013

"Successful people ask better questions, and as a result, they get better answers."

Tony Robbins

QUESTION ONE

Is YouTube Really A Social Network? How Can You Leverage That Fact?

The fact is simple, YouTube is a social network—and you need to plan your approach to YouTube accordingly. How can I say so? YouTube says so and a bunch of other people say so. So let's go further and deconstruct this concept.

What makes a social network? Friends, comments, followers, subscriptions—these are all part of the social network experience, and they are also a part of YouTube.

But she doesn't stand alone. YouTube also (in many ways, uniquely), ties in closely with other social networks. There are feeds of content and activity streams, all the things that make up a social network are inside. It has all of it, so it is completely and totally a social network.

Why would Google make YouTube a social network

when there are so many? There are a couple of reasons that are really simple if you think about them.

Number one, social equals stick. When you come to see the stuff that you've subscribed to, or you come to see stuff that you've commented on, or you've come to see the community that you're integrating with, that is stick. You will stay longer and you will come back. Social is stick.

Stick is more money (for YouTube). The longer the people stay, the more ads YouTube can put up. The more interactivity they can get, the bigger the audience they can build. The more they have the more things they can charge more money for.

So social is stick and stick is more money.

Finally, YouTube quite simply is smart. Having a video replayed, on a page, in a network that isn't social is not going to bring them the revenue that they are looking for. It's not going to put them in the strategic position that they are looking for. Remember, YouTube is very smart and is doing all this on purpose.

Let's take a more in depth look at what social means. I'm sure you know at this point that YouTube is owned by Google. Google is spending a considerable amount of time and money and effort on Google+. Google+ is not a social network, Google+ is a social platform, nicely integrated to YouTube. You should do the same.

So what are the action items? What do you do with this?

Action item number one, treat YouTube as the social network that it is. Make it as much a part of your marketing efforts as is Twitter, Facebook, Google+ and anything else you might be doing.

Number two, do things that will A, bring more viewers as a result of social networking and B, do things that will make YouTube more money. What do I mean by this? YouTube makes more money the more subscribers you have because they come back and they see more videos (YouTube is social). YouTube makes more money the more comments you get, because viewers want to see if somebody commented on their comment (YouTube is social). The more interactivity, the more social inside of YouTube, the more money YouTube makes.

In short, the more you do for YouTube, the more YouTube will do for you.

Part three is get involved inside of Google+. YouTube will leverage the integration to their advantage because…YouTube is Social.

You might have heard Google+ is a ghost town. You might have heard Google+ is not worth utilizing. You might have heard a number of things about Google+.

Whereas some of them may be true, the realization that Google+ is a social platform should direct you to integrate your Google+ account into your YouTube account and let Google do the rest. They do it well, so let them. You'll benefit from it.

So yes, YouTube is very much social network. Yes you can leverage it, and I just showed you how.

Summary

Yes; YouTube is a social network because it has features like friends, comments, subscriptions, interactivity, content feeds, and activity streams. Furthermore, YouTube ties in with other social networks. Google created YouTube as a social network for several reasons:

Social = stick. When site visitors come to view content that they have subscribed to, commented on, or interacted with, they will spend a longer time on the site.

Stick = more money. The longer people stay on your site, the more opportunities you have to show an ad. Also, a bigger audience means YouTube can charge higher rates for advertising space.

Social = smart. YouTube knows that creating a site where people replay videos thousands of times that isn't social won't bring them the revenue that a social, interactive, site could. People simply spend more time on social sites.

Google also created Google+, and while Google+ is not a social network but a social platform, it was designed to integrate with YouTube. Videos that your connections share in your Google+ feed, for example, are automatically available on YouTube.

Action Items

1. Make YouTube part of your marketing efforts, like you already do with Twitter, Facebook, and Google+.

2. Maximize interactivity on your YouTube page to bring more viewers to your page and bring more money for YouTube.

3. Use the Google+ platform (in spite of what you may have heard), and integrate it with YouTube.

QUESTION TWO

How Do I Make The Best Of The New YouTube Live Options?

For those of you who have heard of the YouTube live option, the idea is exciting. Let's take a look at what this means. YouTube has built an element that let's you broadcast live to your YouTube audience.

Think about this ... Imagine telling your audience "you can catch me live on YouTube this Thursday at 8 pm."

At this point in time, the option is open to a small, select group of YouTube partners, and the future of the program is still unknown. In fact, YouTube has said nothing about it over the last six months.

Why has YouTube stayed silent about the live option? Because it has tightly integrated Google hangouts (which are part of Google+) with YouTube channels. All users have the ability to log into their Google+ accounts, have a hangout, and share the hangout with their audience (anybody on the continental U.S., and potentially worldwide) as a video streaming live on their YouTube channel.

So, the good news is that even if the future of YouTube live is uncertain, there is a back door to broadcasting live on YouTube via Google+. (Just search for video walkthroughs or tutorials on how to use Google hangouts to broadcast live.)

Here is a video I did about Hangouts On YouTube: http://www.youtube.com/watch?v=NS-OvKRGIxM

So what are the action items? How can you make the best use of YouTube live?

Number one, utilize this tool in all of your marketing efforts and in everything you do. The ability to say, "Watch me live on YouTube" carries a tremendous amount of cache. Just imagine having the ability to tell your list that you'll be live on YouTube every Friday to answer questions, or on any one day at a specific time. Broadcasting live should definitely be part of your plan.

The second point is that if you do hold a live event and you feel that it didn't go well, know that you can delete any video from your video archive. It's not difficult to do, and it's perfectly natural.

Your third action item is to understand that this is the future of Internet video. Internet video is going live—and the ability to interact, to be social, to ask questions and know that you are in the same time and place as the person consuming the video is what lies ahead. You absolutely need to take part in this, and make it part of your business and marketing. That's how you make best use of the new YouTube live options.

Summary

YouTube now has an element built into the site that allows you to broadcast live to your YouTube audience. Currently, this is available to a small number of YouTube partners. One reason that YouTube has been silent on this new feature is because of its tight integration with Google+, facilitating Google hangouts that can be broadcasted live on your YouTube channel. So, while YouTube Live is only open to a select few and its future is unknown, Google+ Hangouts are a great opportunity to broadcast live.

Action Items

1. Use live broadcasting in your marketing efforts. Being able to say that you'll be available live on YouTube is tremendous, compelling, and should certainly be utilized as part of your communications with your audience.

2. Delete any non-stellar live events that you aren't

pleased with from your archives.

3. Understand that live streaming is the future of video; you need to take part in the transformation. Remember, Internet video gives you the ability to interact with your audience, to be social, and to answer questions live.

QUESTION THREE

How Can I Optimize My YouTube Channel And Videos?

The facts here are simple. Whatever content is being consumed on the Internet at an increasing rate, it's being viewed on mobile devices: mostly over phones, and in some case tablets. Mobile is the fastest growing market for YouTube, as well as the fastest growing market for pretty much anybody. Every batch of statistics point to the same fact: mobile is growing.

The good news is that by default, YouTube has set everything up for mobile compatibility. Your channel and all of your videos are currently ready for mobile—you don't have to do anything.

However you do have to take a couple of things into consideration. Clicks, annotations and ads don't always work as well on mobile devices as they do on desktop computers. What do I mean by that?

Using annotations, ads and descriptions under YouTube

videos, you've seen people say "Click on the links below." If you're watching on a phone, they won't see links below. If you say something like "Click on this annotation," the mobile device interface may or may not show the annotation.

So since clicks, annotations, ads don't always work as well on mobile, your task is to not say or do anything that will make you look silly. Don't call the annotations and links out as a matter of fact, because a lot of people—as a matter of fact, the largest percentage of your audience—won't be able to view them or interact with them.

If you make extended partner status on YouTube, you are given the option to design a mobile site for your channel. As of late, however, YouTube has said very little about what's going to happen to that program—so I wouldn't necessarily count on it.

In summary, the facts about mobile are simple: it's done for you automatically, you don't have to do anything to your videos or channels, just be aware that clicks, annotations and ads won't show up on mobile devices.

What are the action items?

You have three action items. Number one, realize that your videos might be viewed by someone with a two-inch screen. For example, you may have done a screencast of a high definition computer screen that you broadcast on YouTube. (Screencasting is a tremendously profitable element of YouTube, it's growing by leaps and bounds.) If you have someone who is consuming your screencast on a two-inch screen, it may lose all of its effectiveness. If your video has small lettering and titles, or large swooping vistas and really dramatic video shots, that won't come across on a two-inch screen either.

Furthermore, realize that someone watching your content on a two-inch screen won't have the ability to interact with your video. What you want to do is consider opt-in options that don't require this level of interactivity.

For instance, instead of saying "Click to visit my website," you can say out loud, within your video, "Visit my website at www.x.com." Instead of saying "Send me your name and email address to get a report or to get a coupon," you might ask your viewer to text you his or her name and email address.

In short, whenever you add any opt-in mechanisms to your video, just ask yourself: "Will this work for people in front of a computer? Will this work for people in front of a TV set? And, will this work for people in front of a phone?"

Finally, action item number three is if you're going to do a lot of work in a mobile space, work hard to become a YouTube partner so that you can get a mobile optimized channel.

That's how you optimize your YouTube channel and videos for mobile customers.

Summary

DON'T: worry about configuring your channel for mobile devices—YouTube has already done that for you!

The fact is that mobile is the fastest growing market on YouTube; increasingly, people are consuming media on their phones and tablets. Fortunately, YouTube has already configured its site to function perfectly on a mobile device; you don't have to make any special adjustments to your videos or channel.

DO: adjust your calls to action and interactive elements to incorporate actions that mobile users can perform.

There are certain additional features that you should be aware of, that may not function on mobile devices the way they do on a desktop computer. For example, clicks, annotations, and ads aren't always available when viewed on mobile devices. So, avoid explicitly referring to annotations or clicking opportunities in your video: many users won't be able to interact with them, and most likely won't even be able to see them. Fix this discrepancy by adjusting your calls to action to incorporate all user capabilities.

Action Items

1. Account for the fact that people may view your videos on a small, mobile, screen. This is medium is unsuitable for screencasting, titles and text in small print, or videos that try to communicate dramatic shots; none of these translate well to the two-inch format.

2. Tailor your call to action to include emailing, or texting, rather than just clicking for the opt-in. Somebody on a mobile device will not be able to take advantage of clicking on an opt-in, or clicking on a link to a website.

3. Gain trusted YouTube user or partner status, (by working hard to comply with YouTube's rules, occasionally allowing ads in your videos, and maximizing interactivity on your channel) so that you can create your own mobile optimized channel.

QUESTION FOUR

What Can I Do To Maximize My YouTube Channel?

Everybody wants to maximize their YouTube channel—and you should leverage and make use of every tool you have to achieve this purpose.

Fact one is that YouTube wants people who help them build the YouTube brand. What does this mean? When you put a video on YouTube, it means that YouTube basically has given you some free bandwidth and some free storage for your content. At most, there's a logo in the bottom right hand corner of your videos, but it does nothing substantial to build YouTube's brand.

When you send people to your channel to find other videos, to find playlists, to interact with your channel, you're getting your audience to utilize the YouTube interface—which is exactly what YouTube wants. YouTube wants users who help them build their brand. Why? Because the more people come to their site, the more they can charge for advertising. Consequently, the more you have built out your channel, and the more interactivity it brings, the more YouTube will like you and appreciate you as a user.

Let's go more in depth on this concept. When any audience member subscribes to your channel, every time you put up a new video, they are alerted on the home page. This mechanism is actually how YouTube makes the majority of their money. So, when you create a video, it's important to ask the viewer to subscribe to your channel. Then, when you put up a new video, the channel automatically updates and it brings people to your channel page.

You won't get a lot of customization or options on your channel outside of background graphics, but you can do some pretty cool things with that. Let me show you an example: please visit YouTube.com/Colligan, one of my main pages.

Obviously sending someone to an example like this when YouTube changes all the time is almost silly - but I want to give an example here.

You can also notice my background imagery contains a subscribe mechanism: you'll see a picture of my face, my monthly publishing profile, then even my phone number that can get a new visitor into an open series.

I have this channel optimized and colorized to represent

who I am, and what it is that I do. I also have links to my different websites that I'm working with. I've got featured playlists and all sorts of great content that viewers can take a look at. Most importantly, I have simply put an opt-in mechanism in the background that helps me get leads, and it's worked very well for me.

The fact is that YouTube wants people to help them build the brand. If you build out your channel, you build out their brand, they will like you more—and this will be reflected in your rankings and ratings in the search engine.

Let's summarize: when you ask someone to subscribe to your channel, every time you put up a new video, they'll go to the homepage, you'll build out YouTube, and YouTube will see that you are a valuable user. In terms of optimizing your channel, you won't get much customization past the background graphics, but do as much as you can.

What are the action items?

First and foremost, build a channel worth subscribing to. Take some time to think through the process: get a background image, build playlists, collect links, write descriptions, and make it a home page that you can be proud of.

Secondly, always ask people to subscribe to your

channel—this one is huge. When people subscribe to your channel, it builds your YouTube page and it's good for everybody. Don't always play the most recent video in your channel. A lot of people setup the channel so that it plays the most recent video. In some cases that might make sense, but you want to make sure that your most recent video is a proper first introduction to who you are.

Finally, include an opt-in mechanism in the background graphics of your channel. That is how you maximize your YouTube channel.

Summary

It's important to understand that YouTube wants you to optimize your channel. Why? Because YouTube wants you to help them build the YouTube brand. A video that has simply been uploaded on YouTube has nothing more than the YouTube logo. But a channel or video that brings many users to the site, one that inspires comments, likes, interactivity, traffic, and longer visits is what ultimately build the YouTube brand and bring YouTube more revenue. Most importantly, a popular channel with a large, interactive audience allows YouTube to charge more for advertising space. If you build your channel and give YouTube the traffic it desires, YouTube will appreciate you as a user, and increase your search ranking.

In order to maximize the effectiveness of your YouTube

Channel you need to first take advantage of the customization options, though limited, that YouTube already gives you. You can change the color of the page, as well as your background graphics. Here, make sure you take advantage of this space by including information about yourself, opt-in information, a website URL, and anything that communicates your brand. YouTube also allows you to create playlists and list any links or websites that you're associated with. Use all of these tools to build your channel, optimize your page to suit your brand, and get additional leads through an opt-in mechanism.

Action Items

1. Build a channel worth subscribing to: create a background image, build playlists, and add links.

2. Ask people to subscribe to your channel. (You'd be surprised how many people forget to ask.)

3. Don't make your most recent video as the first video that visitors to your channel see, unless you feel it is a good introduction to who you are.

4. Include an opt-in mechanism on your channel's page.

Special Note

The week this book went to press, YouTube changed their Channel format, again, in some very exciting ways. Although these changes aren't reflected in this book, the special offer I placed at the beginning of this book includes an hour plus long video about what to do and think about the new YouTube OneChannel program.

QUESTION FIVE

How Should I Integrate My YouTube Strategies With Other Social Networks?

Fact one, YouTube has done a tremendous job integrating with other social media, and it's definitely something that you want to leverage. At the time of this writing, YouTube integrates with Google+, Twitter, Facebook and Orkut. That will probably change in the future, but the concepts below are true no matter what the list may hold.

What's interesting is for people who have connected their YouTube accounts with Google+, Twitter, Facebook and Orkut, many social things will happen automatically. For example, if you have linked your YouTube channel to a Twitter account, and someone who has also linked their YouTube account to a Twitter account gives your video a thumbs up, that thumbs up will be published via Twitter. On my YouTube homepage, you'll see that Google+ videos show up. For example, we have somebody who liked a video right inside of YouTube and you can see the "+1" here. The integration is very impressive, very powerful, and something you will definitely want to play with.

YouTube performs a lot of functions by default. You can integrate Google+, Twitter, Facebook, and Orkut automatically. That's done simply by clicking on the social button over on the left hand side. You can see when you click on that, it shows you how you are currently logged in, and you can choose the accounts that you want to be logged in with.

Google+ is automatic and automated, so absolutely utilize it. This connection will help you in search, with social media integration, and with a number of other things.

Twitter makes a lot of sense to integrate with YouTube as well. Orkut only makes sense if your audience is part of the Orkut community. Facebook can only function as your personal Facebook account, and not necessarily your corporate Facebook page. So the integration there is something that you might want to examine further to decide if Facebook integration will be strategic for you.

What are the action items?

First, simply tie in what makes sense. Obviously, since Google+ and Twitter integrate automatically, those two are an easy decision. Remember, for every YouTube channel you have you should have a Twitter page.

Facebook, at this point in time however, only functions with personal account integration. In most cases, when you're using YouTube for marketing purposes, integrating with your personal account won't make sense for your business. YouTube and Facebook will probably solve this fairly soon, however. Integrate with Orkut only if it makes sense for your audience. If you don't know what Orkut is, don't worry about it.

Simply use Google+ with YouTube for tight social integration, and turn on the social integration for tools such as Twitter and Facebook. Realize again that YouTube itself is its own social network, so thinking social and setting things up to be social would be of tremendous value to you. That is how you integrate YouTube with other social media networks.

Summary

YouTube has done an incredible job integrating with other social media sites: at this point in time, Google+, Twitter, Facebook, and Orkut. Certain sites will even automate social news and posts and sync their activity with YouTube's activity. For example, if you link a YouTube Channel to a Twitter account, and somebody has liked a video on your YouTube Channel, the news will automatically publish to your Twitter feed.

The Good News: Google+ and YouTube already automatically integrate and work together beautifully.

Google+ automatically integrates, so make sure that you take advantage of this tool. Linking a YouTube Channel with Facebook, however, would link to your personal account, and that may or not be strategic for you. Another great feature inside of YouTube is that once you've linked with your Google+, Twitter, Facebook, and/or Orkut accounts, you can choose which account you want to log into and browse YouTube with.

Action Items

1. Tie in the social media accounts that make sense for you and your business.

2. Don't hesitate to integrate Google+; it's automatic, and creates seamless integration.

3. Create a YouTube Channel for every Twitter Page, and vice versa.

4. You can only integrate Facebook via a personal account, so at this point in time know that this option may or may not be optimal for your business;

5. Use Orkut if it makes sense: only if your audience and/or target demographic are using the social network.

QUESTION SIX

How Do You Get Your YouTube Video Ranked On The Front Page Of Google?

How do you get your video arranged on the first page of Google results? This one is a lot easier than a lot of pundits would like to make it out be. If you understand the following simple concepts, you can do tremendously well with YouTube and Google results.

Fact number one is that Google is in the business of delivering results. If they don't deliver good results, people will leave them: that's their number one job.

Number two, Google has a massive staff of people whose job is to defeat users trying to trick the results. Obviously, a lot of people who shouldn't be the number one listing for a given search result, still want to be the number one listing. There is a whole industry of search engine optimization (SEO), where experts in Google teach people how to manipulate the search engine. Fortunately, Google has hired a substantial staff of very brilliant people—and I've met some of them personally, PhD's,

Gurus and brainy people—whose job is simply to screen anybody who's playing tricks.

So tricks can happen, but realize that it is a considerable cat and mouse game that I don't recommend playing in any way, shape, or form.

Also realize that Google likes video better than anything else. Think about it, if a given search produces results, and one of these results is YouTube, that's a video that's going to get long engagement. The video result is going to get the viewer to stay on the site, and potentially give way to showing that viewer an ad. Google loves video results, which is exactly what you have. You're at a good place.

Now something that not everybody realizes, is that YouTube tracks how long people watch each video. In other words, 10,000 views of a five-minute video where everybody leaves after the first ten seconds of the video, indicates to YouTube that 10,000 people didn't believe this to be a good video about the topic at hand. Fifty people who watched the entire video is considerably better—even five people who watched the entire video is considerably better than 10,000 who stopped after a few seconds.

So Google wants to give its users good results, and it knows whether or not a result is good based on how long people spend watching the video. If people watched the video all the way through, Google will decide this was an appropriate result for the keywords searched. It's as simple as that.

What can you do?

Make the best video for the Google results, to reach an audience who is going to consume the content all the way to the end. If you do that better than anybody else does, you will get ranked on the first page of Google results. That process is actually much easier than cheating the system and playing SEO games.

In fact, I have videos three years old that are still number one for the results, still getting hundreds of views a week because they were optimized for that keyword. They are only going to do better because we have the longevity of the video.

Google is in the business of getting results and they have a massive staff whose job is to identify people who are trying to trick them. They track how long people watch each video and they know how good the video is based how long it has been watched. In short, create the best choice for the audience and Google will put you first.

What are the action items?

First, the title for your video should include the keyword that people are looking for. The keyword also needs to be in the description of the video, the tags for the video, and the transcript of the video.

Next, you need to make sure that you have a video that people watch all the way through. To track those statistics, look inside your YouTube handle. For each video you will see how long people watch, and you'll see when they drop off as compared to everybody else. If you've got a great video with a key word rich title, description, transcript, and tags, but you notice that people aren't watching it all the way through to the end, fix your video by adjusting your content. If you do that and you will see some great results and you will see your video on the first page of Google search results.

Summary

Contrary to popular belief, it is not too difficult to get your videos ranked high in a Google search. You need to understand that Google is in the business of delivering results; if they don't deliver good results, they'll lose their users. Furthermore, there is an enormous staff of brilliant programmers dedicated to preventing non-deserving first page rankings. Though there is a massive SEO industry, with its own strategies that may or may not be effective, Google is putting forth a considerable effort to defeat people who are trying to beat the game in an unauthentic way.

The Bottom Line: Google is in the business of delivering results.

Google loves video results, because it loves sending people to YouTube where they can receive sustained engagement from their viewers. Most importantly, YouTube tracks not only the number of views that your videos get, but the length of time that people spend watching your videos. For example, 10,000 views on a five minute video where viewers become disengaged and leave after five seconds indicates that people didn't think that the video addressed the issue, or gave them the result they wanted. Since Google wants good results for people who search on their site, they track these metrics and steer away from videos that clearly weren't satisfying to their viewers.

The Bottom Line: Not all views are equal; Google values videos that people watch from beginning to end.

Your job is to provide videos that your audience wants to watch, and do it better than anybody else does. The fact is that creating honestly good, valuable, and relevant content is easier than trying to beat the game by manipulating SEO.

Action Items

1. Include the searchable key words in your video's title, in the description of the video, in tags for the video, as well as the transcript of your video.

2. Create content that is relevant and compelling, so

that people watch your videos to the end, rather than leaving after several seconds. You can check YouTube's metrics to see how long people engage with your videos; if you notice they aren't watching the entire video, adjust your content.

QUESTION SEVEN

What Are The Best SEO Methods And Strategies For A YouTube Video?

What are the best SEO methods for a YouTube video? What can you do, once you're put your video online, to give it the best possibility of getting found?

The facts are, we know that YouTube looks for the topic of your video to be in each of the following aspects of your video: the title (if someone is looking for content about a topic, that topic better be in the title), the description, the keywords, and the transcripts. If at all possible, it would be of extra value to you to include the topic inside of the channel name too.

Let me give you an example. If you have a channel called "Colligan" that features yoga videos, there is no real connection between Colligan and yoga videos. (Especially, if you know me in any way shape or form.) But a yoga video and a channel called "Free Yoga Videos" makes a lot of sense. And, getting multiple channels that match up with your content might be something that is worth considering.

So, to recap, include the topic in the title, the description, the keywords, the transcripts, and the channel name if at all possible.

We know Google (who owns YouTube) tracks links and the keywords associated with them. It would be incredibly valuable for you in your YouTube video SEO strategy to include keywords in the link that takes people to your videos. For example, if you have a video called "Free Yoga Workout Video," the link should be called "Free Yoga Workout Video." This is what Google looks for—and it makes sense.

Another SEO method is embedding videos on sites about that topic. If you embed a YouTube video about yoga (with the a topic rich description, title, transcript, keywords, and channel name) on a website about yoga, Google is going to know that your video is a match for that topic.

And think about it, if you have a video and several relevant websites contain the link about your topic, doesn't that start to come together for you quite nicely?

Finally, have a video that people watch to the end. This is a tremendous issue. YouTube tracks how far people watch their videos. If you setup the title, the description, the keywords, the transcripts, the channel name, the links, and the site the video is embedded about a certain topic, but people don't watch the video to the end— Google will know that you are playing a game. But if you're video is watched to the end, it doesn't matter how much optimization you do, at the end they are not going to link to you accordingly.

What are your action items for optimization?

Number one, figure out the keywords that you want to be found for. Once you decide the keywords that you're looking to be found for inside of YouTube, realize that will let you build everything out accordingly. A lot of people want to be found for X, but they make a video about Y. They realize they want to be found for X, so they could integrate X into that video, even if that video is a little bit Y.

Again, remember you want them to watch the video through to the end. Design a video that will be watched through to the end that contains those keywords, and now you have Google validating your work as in fact being viable and valuable.

Next, make sure the keywords are everywhere they can be—that's of incredible value to you.

Get the video embedded on sites about that topic. If you're marketing on YouTube about a certain topic I'm going to guess that you probably have sites related to that topic. You might want to work with co-authors and competitors if necessary.

Finally, get links with the keywords that you're looking for from sites containing the keywords to your YouTube video. Those are the best SEO methods for your YouTube video.

Summary

For optimal results on Google and YouTube, make sure that the topic of your video—that is, the words that your audience will be searching for—is contained in each of the following aspects of your video:

- In the title of your video

- In the description of your video

- In the transcript of your video

- In the tags for your video

- (Bonus Points) Inside of your channel's name

- In the links to your video

For example, if you want to create a channel dedicated to yoga videos, make sure to give it a name that explicitly states the topic such as "Free Yoga Videos." Making all of these elements keyword rich will make it clear to Google that the video is relevant to users searching for that topic. For the optimal situation, you can embed your keyword rich YouTube video on a website with the appropriate URL, for example, Freeyogavideos.com.

However, even if you've done all of this search engine optimization but at the end of it all, your audience simply doesn't watch your videos to the end, Google will realize that you are playing a game rather than providing top-notch content. In other words, it won't validate your work as viable and valuable. Conversely, even if you haven't optimized your video but viewers love and watch your content, Google will link it and rank it accordingly.

Action Items

1. Determine the keywords that people will be searching for, relevant to your topic.

2. Create content that's relevant to your keyword, and design it in a way that people who searched for that topic will want to watch your video to the end.

3. Include keywords in every place you can, from the title of the video, to the title of the channel.

4. Embed the video on sites relevant to its topic; work with coauthors or experts in your field if you need to.

5. Get links with keywords that you're looking for from sites containing the keywords to your YouTube video.

QUESTION EIGHT

What Equipment And Software Do I Need To Create A Decent Quality Video?

First, you need a high definition camera. Funny thing is the high definition camera on your phone is probably good enough for what you need to do. And while the HD camera on your phone is good, you can get many for less than $100.

Actually, more important than the video is the audio quality. I've seen people who have $50 phone cameras, but $200, $400 audio rigs because the audio is actually more important than the HD image quality.

Do you need that high definition camera? Yes, you do, because you want to upload in high definition quality to YouTube so that they take you seriously (but audio is still more important.) There are several great microphones for under $100—and you can do your homework by visiting a site like Amazon and looking for the most highly ranked equipment.

The next most important thing is the lighting: you want to have great lighting. There is what they call the industry three-point lighting, which you can search for in your favorite search engine. (YouTube has video after video that explains how to utilize this method.)

One alternative, if you don't have good lighting, is to go outside to Mother Nature where there is good lighting. (Obviously, don't go out shooting in the middle of a storm.) But know that lighting is the second most important aspect of your video production.

A descent quality video can also be a screencasted video. The video that I created for this content (the video that this ebook is based on) is a screencasted video that's been extremely profitable for me. With screencasting, I don't have to worry about lighting, I don't have to worry about cameras, I just need software and a microphone.

The microphone I use is the Blue Yeti, purchased for under $100 on Amazon. In terms of screencasting programs, there you have two software options: Camtasia on the PC and ScreenFlow on the Mac. Both of those programs have 30-day trials that you can utilize if you need, and you can produce great videos with them. They even have the ability to input video editing if that's something you need.

Finally, in terms of traditional video editing, iMovie on the Mac works well. Whatever version of iMovie you have is great, and you can download it from the Apple store. If you are unfortunate and saddled with a PC, I would not recommend Windows Movie Maker. Sony Vegas on the PC, however, is a fine product—and you can usually get that with a coupon for under $100.

So the action item is simply to get over the tech, grab a high definition camera for under $100, and realize that most likely, your phone will do the job.

Next, invest in descent audio, set up quality lighting, and get to work on making your videos. Then put them on YouTube and see what kind of response you get. There is no better way to buy a new camera than from the success of your previous videos.

That's all the equipment and software you need to make a descent quality video. Get to work.

Summary

To create a high quality video, the first thing you'll need is a high definition camera—not unlike the one that you might have on your phone. If you decide you want something higher quality than the camera on your phone, you can purchase an HD camera for less than $100. To ensure professional image quality, it's imperative that you use proper lighting. You can use the industry three-point lighting for best results, or alternatively, rely on natural lighting outdoors.

<u>The Common Pitfall</u>: Don't spend all your energy on a great image; ultimately, good, clean audio is more important.

However, realize that audio quality is even more important than picture quality. You can purchase a great microphone for under $100, such as the Blue Yeti. If you want to create videos without using a camera, or without starring in front of a camera, you can utilize screencasting. Using softwares like Camtasia for the PC or ScreenFlow for the Mac, you can capture your screen as you go through a Keynote or Powerpoint presentation, or the like.

When you're in the final stage of editing your videos, you can accomplish everything you need inside of iMovie if you use a Mac. If you use a PC, steer clear of Windows Movie Maker, but you can use Sony Vegas and usually find it for under $100.

Action Items

1. Purchase a decent high definition camera for $100 or less, or use your phone if it has an HD camera built in.

2. Shoot videos in proper lighting. *Recommended: 3-point lighting or natural light.*

3. (Optional) Use screencasting to capture your

screen and bypass the use of a camera. *Recommended: ScreenFlow for Mac and Camtasia for PCs*

4. Purchase a quality microphone for under $100 or less to produce great audio. *Recommended: The Blue Yeti*

5. Purchase editing software, to make simple edits and export your final product. *Recommended: iMovie for Macs and Sony Vegas for PCs*

QUESTION NINE

What Value Is There In Closed Captioning Your YouTube Videos?

Now, understand that YouTube actually does automatic closed captioning. At this point in time, they provide it for English as well as a couple other languages. They generate it automatically utilizing the same technology that they utilize in the Google voice product.

Which means, at least the time of this writing, their closed captioning is terrible.

So, they will do automatic close captioning but it's really bad. (I've almost wanted to dedicate a channel about the bad closed captioning that comes from Google and YouTube—because it's just absolutely terrible.)

With the way this technology is going and the nuances of close captioning videos, I honestly don't see it improving for many years. However, YouTube does search through the closed captioning and they will show results accordingly.

Think about it: a 15-minute video might have a lot of words in it. But somebody searching for a certain term or phrase might find it in minute seven within that video. The good news is, YouTube will offer you the ability to go right to that part of the video within the search results. That capability is quite profound and shows how feverously integrated YouTube and Google really are.

Also, realize that instead of just optimizing your video with the title, description, tags and links, you can actually optimize your video so that every single word said within the video also contains keywords. Scripting your video suddenly begins to make sense—and you can totally use this to your advantage.

What's interesting is outside of search, there are actually some additional advantages to optimizing your video's closed captioning. Realize that there is a tremendous audience of people who can't hear or are unable to consume audio. If you have close captioning for your videos, you have suddenly given that demographic the ability to consume your videos.

What's also interesting is that there are a number of people who want to watch videos without disturbing others—whether they are at work, on a bus, or on some sort of transport where having their audio go out loud might get them into trouble. The bottom line: if you've got close captioning you might get video consumption that you wouldn't get otherwise.

At this point Google does not provide search through the transcripts—but let's think about this. Google owns YouTube, YouTube searches the transcripts, why in the world wouldn't they tie those two together? So, though at this point Google doesn't search the transcripts, logically, it has to be coming soon.

Finally, if you do put together a transcript, you can upload it inside of YouTube. You can also make content from that transcript, and put that content up on your blog. Now, every key word becomes searchable by Google.

What are your action items for closed captioning?

In the best case scenario, get all your videos transcribed, and upload the transcripts for each video. People always want to know, who is a good transcriptionist? At the time of this recording, there is a very cool service called VoiceText.com. They will do things automatically, you can actually just pay them to go in and do transcripts for all the videos on your channel. And their results are pretty accurate, and quite impressive.

Your middle case is to at least edit the text within the closed captioning, and make sure that it captures the keywords correctly. If you do that, you'll get a slight bump—nothing like what you get with full transcripts—but editing is an option.

Understand that there is definite value in close captioning

your YouTube videos. If you're going to play serious, you might want to consider going all the way.

Summary

Google will search for keywords in closed captioning.

YouTube creates automatic closed captioning, for English as well as several other languages, but at this point in time the captioning is incredibly inaccurate. However, the value of closed captioning is that YouTube will search for keywords or phrases within the text. For example, if somebody searches for a particular search and finds it within your video, YouTube will offer that person the ability to jump straight to that part of the video. What are the implications of this tool? You can strategize not only your titles and descriptions, but your spoken video content—and it will pay off to meticulously script your videos.

You'll be able to reach a wider audience.

In addition to the search and search ranking advantages, closed captioning allows you to reach an audience that you may not have otherwise been able to reach. For example, people who are hearing impaired, people who wish to watch your video without audio because they are in a public space, or people who are unable to hear the audio in their setting, can suddenly still consume your video by reading the subtitles. Finally, you can upload a transcript with your YouTube video, then post the transcript to your blog, making each keyword searchable.

Action Items

1. Get your videos transcribed, and upload them to YouTube. To find a good transcriptionist, you can use a service called VoiceText.com.

2. Edit the transcript created within YouTube, if you don't upload your own transcript, to make sure the key words are included correctly.

QUESTION TEN

What Is The Ideal Length For A YouTube Video?

People ask this all the time: what is the ideal video length? You hear stories that, "We are in the YouTube era, nobody watches video more than three minutes." People make these blanket statements of absolute pure nonsense, so let's take the time to walk through these myths.

Fact one, *the concept that people only watch short videos online is simply false.*

If you think about it logically, YouTube has spent millions of dollars putting up full-length concerts, all day festivals, and all day events; people consume long form content. They also put up a lot of political events, speeches, debates that are all consumed in great quantities. YouTube would not spend millions putting up long form content if people didn't watch it.

The reason why most videos are only three minutes in length, is because most people only have three minutes of content to say. Or, they are building videos for an audience with three minute attention spans. If you only have three minutes of content to say, and you have an audience with a three-minute attention span, obviously deal with that audience—but the idea that only short videos are consumed is absolutely ridiculous.

So what is the ideal video length? How long should you make your video?

The answer is actually quite simple: make your video as long as it needs to be and not one minute more. The fact of the matter is, you have to know your audience. You have to know what it is they are looking for, and you have to deliver the content that you have. Realize they can click out, they can go anywhere they want, and that there are competitors to the very piece of information you are trying to portray on YouTube. For that reason, the video needs to be as long as it needs to be not one minute—actually, not one second—more.

So what are the action items? What can you do?

It's an interesting era that we are in—with massive hard drives, unlimited upload space, and the ability to send hours of video to YouTube—and we do tend to go longer than we need to. Your action item is easy: don't.

When producing your video, figure exactly what you have to say, and more importantly, figure out exactly what you don't need to say. Then, say only what it is that you need to say, and say it very quickly.

Also, what happens after a video is consumed? Make that part of the content, but again, do that quickly.

Another tip for you is to tell your viewer how long your video is up front—it helps tremendously. What would you rather watch, a video called "Social Media Marketing" or a video called "Social Media Marketing Explained in 3 Minutes and 7 Seconds?" Think about it, I got three minutes so I'll give that. So it can be a strategic implementation—but don't worry about going longer if you need to.

Summary

One common but false belief about videos is that since we are in the "YouTube era," people will not watch videos longer than three minutes in length. This is an inaccurate, blanket statement. YouTube spends millions on providing full-length concerts, all day events, and speeches on its site—and YouTube certainly wouldn't do this if people weren't watching the content.

The reason behind this perception is that most people only have three minutes worth of content, or are trying to communicate with an audience that has a three minute attention span. The crucial factor is that you understand your audience, and understand what your audience needs and wants to hear from you. So how long does your video need to be? The answer is simple: your video needs to be as long as it needs to be to communicate your content effectively, and give the viewer what he or she was looking for, and not one minute longer.

The Bottom Line: The video needs to be as long as it needs to be, and not one second more.

Action Items

1. Determine exactly what you need to say and what you don't need to say, and say exactly that in your video.

2. Tell your audience how long your video or content is going to be in the beginning of your video, or even in the title or description of your video. They'll appreciate it!

QUESTION ELEVEN

How Should I Use YouTube Annotations?

You've probably seen YouTube annotations: pop ups, text bubbles, links, all in different colors and fonts, and all part of the YouTube system. YouTube is working diligently, spending millions of dollars to integrate this across all the platforms such as television and mobile.

What do you do with that, how do you use them, how do you make them part of your business?

Number one, annotations bring integration, they bring interactivity, and they bring some very cool things into the online video process. You definitely want to leverage that.

Fact number two, YouTube is adding more and more features, they are taking it very seriously, and as I mentioned earlier, they are working diligently in making it work across all their platforms. YouTube is focused on letting you do more cool things on more platforms with them.

Some people won't be able to see or interact with annotations, however, so you need to keep that in consideration. Realize that right now, at least at the time of this writing, you can even add an annotation that says, "Click here to get a million dollars," but if that person is watching on an iPhone, they won't see the annotation, and won't click for the cash. People on mobile devices just aren't able to use annotations, so take that in consideration during the production of your videos.

So what can you do with annotations? You can obviously incorporate humor, as well as commentary, and supplemental things that aren't necessary. You can ask somebody to subscribe or make a joke by telling them when the next video is coming out. Annotations that work best are ones have no negative impact if they are not seen (like when they're viewed on mobile or another screen.)

One thing you can do is you can link—and that's a powerful side of annotations. At the time of this writing, you can link to other YouTube videos. Imagine that somebody has just found you, they're watching a video that they like, so when they reach the end of the video and they want more, you should certainly tell them, "I have more, here's a video about X." The great thing is that when viewers click on an annotation, it takes them right to that video.

I've seen people who have added annotations to their videos and doubled their viewing just over the course of the week.

You can also link to a playlist, simply by saying, "If you like this video, I've got ten more videos on this topic," and provide a link to that list. Realize too, the playlist can come up in YouTube results, so you have double power there.

You can also link viewers back to your channel page. By providing a channel link, you link people back to who it is you are and what it is you do: it's very powerful, very easy, and I definitely recommend you do that.

You can add an annotation to a Google+ profile page. In fact, Google Talk, Google, YouTube, Google Docs—all of the Google empire—tightly integrate with the Google+ social platform. So if you build the link outside of YouTube to your Google+ profile page, it is incredibly powerful. It will bring people to additional content, additional sites and there, you can link to a subscription button.

Getting people to subscribe to your YouTube channel is incredibly beneficial and something that you want to consider; the more people subscribed, the more people will come back when you put up the next video. It begins to be a snowball rolling down the side of the mountain— it's gets bigger and bigger with the power of gravity that comes along with it.

You can also link to a fundraising project for non-profits or to a Kickstarter account. And finally, to traditional merchandise providers. YouTube has a list of ones that you can use, so do check the list. So, you can link to many cool things, just be aware of the people who can't view them.

What are the action items? What can you do with all these choices?

Make use of annotations when they make sense. For example, including a subscribe annotation in every single one of your videos makes complete and total sense. Let people know that you've got more for them to see by linking to playlists and linking to other videos—all of those are very strategic and very easily implemented. They don't know you, they don't know that you have this other video, so linking those things can be incredibly powerful.

If you're linked to something external, speak to the fact that it might know work on their particular screen and give them an alternative.

For example, you might have the video and say "To learn more, go ahead and click on the link that says learn more and we'll take it right out to an account over at Kickstarter. Or if you're viewing on a phone or a television set or something that doesn't have external links you can visit us at Kickstarter.com," and then put that link right inside of the video. Linking to something external and speaking to it fine, you just need to speak to the fact that they might not be able to do that as well.

Finally, annotations asking people to give you the thumbs up are always doable. Of course, you make it social, and you get automatic sharing across to all the different networks. That is your best use of YouTube annotations.

Summary

A. What do YouTube annotations offer?

You've probably seen them pop up as you're watching videos: text bubbles, links, ads, in different colors and different fonts. How can you use them in your business? Annotations give you several great capabilities: integration and interactivity. However, keep in mind that while YouTube is working diligently to improve these tools, at this point in time, people viewing your videos on mobile devices will miss your annotations and pop ups.

B. What should I include in my annotations?

- ❖ Add humor

- ❖ Write commentary

- ❖ Ask viewers to subscribe

❖ Direct viewers towards other videos on the topic

❖ Link viewers to a playlist

❖ Link viewers to a channel

❖ Link to a fundraising project (such as Kick Starter)

❖ Link to traditional merchandise providers

Annotations are tightly integrated with the entire Google empire: Google+, Google, YouTube, and Google Docs. Therefore, if you add an annotation to your Google+ profile page, it will bring people to additional content and can also lead them to subscribe to your YouTube page. Use annotations to capture and redirect your YouTube traffic to other sites, links, or channels, but also, use them to enhance the viewing experience with humor, commentary.

Action Items

1. Include a "Subscribe" annotation in every single one of your videos to encourage people to subscribe to your YouTube channel.

2. Use annotations to provide links to other sites or videos if applicable.

3. Explicitly state where you want to redirect your

viewer if you do link to an external site or video. Also know that somebody on a mobile device probably cannot access the annotation.

4. Make annotations social by activating the automatic sharing facilitated by Google+.

QUESTION TWELVE

How Do I Make My Video Go "Viral?"

Everybody dreams of making their videos viral. A couple of simple facts you should know. Number one, thinking your video is going to be viral is an absolutely terrible strategy. You've heard the number of hours of content uploaded to YouTube every minute. How many of them are viral? Such a minimal amount.

The chances for you to make your video viral is infinitesimally small; it is a terrible strategy.

Now if for some reason, at some point your video becomes viral, if a zillion people downloaded it, great, leverage it, take hold of it. But the chances of that are up there with you winning the lottery. It is very hard to plan a viral video, it's just something that you just have to know how to do.

Also, viral videos tend not to be marketing videos. Viral videos tend not to be anything that makes anybody money, there may be song rights that come there. Really not much bang for the buck in viral video anyway, other than simply the bragging rights.

I once spoke at an event a copy of one of my YouTube products. It was a drawing type of thing for people who attended. There were two people who said, "We need this so badly," and they were the people behind a viral video that had millions of views. They had barely seen a dime for it. So don't do that, don't go there.

In truth, here is what makes a viral video, it's not complicated:

A viral video is a video where somebody goes, "I have got to share this." That's the video that creates that visceral response where you just have to share it.

What are the things that people have to share? They have to share really one thing, and that is something entirely unexpected. If they come to YouTube, they see a video they are expecting to see. But if you get them something entirely different than everything else, then you've got a chance that they'll share it.

There are two ways that this happens. One—like a good majority of viral videos—is just humor. People love to be the one that forwards along the joke. One of your best chances to at least add some viral elements to it is just by adding humor.

The other reason that people pass along is something I've learned from my friend Tim Street, (video web guy, extraordinaire.) Tim says that viral comes from the mixing of two separate contrasting emotions. Think about it, you've seen videos where it's a serene, beautiful moment and then something scary jumps out. Or ones where it's a humorous moment that gets tragic very quickly. Anything where you have contrasting emotions—tragic meets comedic, beautiful meets ugly—that gets videos to go viral because it's something people don't see coming. The shock value that comes from that forces them to pass that along, so that's where viral comes from.

What are the action items?

Action number one is very simple: don't worry about going viral, you're not going to do that.

It is a really bad strategy despite what I explained here. Instead, worry about matching your video message to your audience, worry about making a video that says what it is that you want to say to the audience that needs to hear it.

Remember, if you have a bunch of folks watching the video for only a few seconds, YouTube simply won't give your video the search-ability or findability. Find people who actually are interested in what it is that you have to say.

To confirm and reiterate, don't worry about making things viral, it's really just a bad strategy to sink your teeth into. It's a bit of "hopium" if you will. Work on a video that people will consume so that YouTube knows you're real about what it is that you're doing.

Sorry to burst your bubble, but that's the sobering truth on making your video viral.

Summary

Creating a viral video is everyone's dream, in this day and age. The truth is, going after the viral video is a terrible and usually fruitless strategy. If you take into account the number of videos, and the hours of footage, that are uploaded daily, the odds of creating a viral video are slim to none.

The Bottom Line: Don't waste your time trying to make a viral video.

So where do viral videos come from? At the core of the viral video phenomenon is the element of surprise. Videos that manage to go viral and receive millions and millions of views are ones that were shared over and over again because each viewer found something unexpected in that video. And while a majority of these videos involve humor, another essential factor is that viral videos mix two dramatically contrasting emotions. For example, a great viral video links the beautiful and the horrifying, the tragic and the humorous, and so on.

Action Items

1. Don't worry about going viral; it's a bad strategy.

2. Do worry about matching your video content to your market; create a message that your audience wants to hear.

QUESTION THIRTEEN

What Quality Should I Publish My YouTube Videos In?

There are a lot of people who love to get techy, nerdy, distracted with their videos' optimum bit rate and functional rate. In spite of all that, it's really simple: YouTube will take whatever it can possibly get and will do everything it can to make it look as awesome as possible.

They've got brilliant people who have been put on this task. So, YouTube can handle better quality than you could have possibly seen anywhere. Just publish at the best possible quality and they'll do the work with everything else. YouTube can dumb it down for people with slow computers, phones with small screens, etc. Just send whatever you've got in the highest possible quality.

What about format...X? Format X works great. YouTube takes it all, that's part of the beauty of what YouTube does.

Also remember that when you send them a YouTube video, this content is going to be up for years. If you do it right, you want a video that has a shelf live of four, six, seven, ten years. Giving them a low quality video right now might be possible now, but what's going to happen in ten years?

YouTube over time is extremely powerful, so you want to do everything you can to upload the video that doesn't just look good now, but that looks good as far into the future as possible. And again, realize that YouTube does all the downgrading and all the cross grading, so you don't have to worry about that.

What are your action items?

Action item number one, really the only one, is publish all videos at the best possible quality you can. YouTube does 1080P or high definition. At the very minimum send them 720P, or standard definition, and 1080P, high definition, if at all possible.

If you own a retina Mac and you've got a video editing station that can produce even higher than 1080P, go ahead and do send them that; YouTube can handle it and it will last you longer down the road.

Do remember that some people are watching videos on mobile phone screens. Although you send YouTube a massive file—one that shows the flies on the back of the horses as they are running through the fields in crystal clarity—not everybody will be able to watch in that sort of definition. Send the high quality video, but develop a video that still looks good if consumed on a screen that's no bigger than a couple square inches.

So again, publish all the videos at the best possible quality you can: 720 at the bare minimum, and 1080 if at all possible. If you could do even better, absolutely do it. But then, despite all the quality, remember that some people are consuming videos on small screens with slow connectivity—so plan your content accordingly.

Summary

If you're interested in technology and video formatting, you may know that there are a number of different options—optimum bit rates, functional rates, etc.—that you can choose from when exporting your video. However, you can trust that YouTube will take whatever video you give it and make it look as beautiful as possible. Send in the best quality that you have, and let YouTube worry about the rest.

The Good News: YouTube wants to make your videos look as good as possible.

Whatever you post to YouTube will be up for years; make sure that it's a format that will age gracefully and will still look great after several more years of innovation. Let

YouTube worry about adjusting your format across platforms, and downgrading the quality if it needs to.

The Bottom Line: Publish all videos at the best possible quality you can.

Action Items

1. Publish all videos at the best quality you can. YouTube does stream at 1080P quality, so if possible, provide 1080P (HD quality), and nothing lower than 720P (DVD quality).

2. Consider viewers streaming on a two-inch screen and plan your visuals accordingly. Though YouTube will downsize the video and optimize it for a smaller screen, it's up to you to make sure the images still communicate your message effectively.

QUESTION FOURTEEN

How Do I Get My Videos To Link Outside Of YouTube?

YouTube doesn't make it easy to link your videos outside of YouTube because of the damage that could come from this. Think about it, anybody can upload to YouTube, and they can upload anything they want. If they promise a website that sends people to a malware site or sends people to spyware, the amount of damage that could be done quickly is something that YouTube has to be incredibly cautious of.

So YouTube doesn't make this easy because of the potential damage.

This is one of those times it's worth being a YouTube partner and working to have a tight relationship. They have let people who have performed extremely well link external to their YouTube videos (in rare circumstances.) If this is something valuable to you, you are going to have to do well—we are talking thousands and thousands of views, and something that you're not going to get just by asking for it.

However, there are ways anybody can get a link external.

Number one, just ask for the link inside of the video, you'd be surprised how easy this is and how well it works. Just say in your video, "Visit my website at www.x.com." If you could also include the text "Visit my website at www.x.com," or wear a t-shirt or a hat with the URL, that works surprisingly well and translates fabulously across all devices.

Again, realize you might have a video that YouTube allows you to provide an external link on. But if someone is watching on their phone or their Xbox, they can't click on the link. So sometimes, it's about integrating the link into the video and asking people to visit the link within your content.

Another thing you can do is include the link within your description. When you put the link inside of the description for your YouTube video, and you write it as http://www.x.com, YouTube will hyperlink that for you. In fact, there have been incredible results that have come from that. Realize again, people viewing from mobile devices or televisions might not have that opportunity. So don't make that the only place that you include the external link.

You can buy ads in front of Ads.YouTube.com, but again,

those only work with the system that supports that, so don't rely on that method entirely.

Inside of an annotation link, and again not being able to view on all the platforms, you can link to other videos outside of YouTube: you can link to playlists inside of YouTube, to channels inside of YouTube, or to a Google+ profile page.

Some people have treated that as the "getting away with murder clause." It's not—it's two clicks away. To send somebody to a profile, then get them to go to something else, is something that you want to think through strategically and figure out if that makes sense for you. It's not always as sexy as it seems. Realize it's more of an issue of Google+ not giving you a back door, as much as it is Google+ having you send people over to Google+.

You can link an annotation to a subscription, which is great. As people consume more content, they get updates when you post more content. You could do it with fundraising projects and you could do it to merchandise—primarily meant for bands and artists—but there are some interesting opportunities inside of that that you should consider and take a look at.

What are the action items for getting your videos to link outside of YouTube?

Number one, do as many of these things as possible.

Definitely make it part of the video, definitely make it part of the description. Make it part of the annotation if that makes sense but in addition to that, make it clear why you want them to leave. To just say "Visit my website for X," in reality won't work. Why? Because I'm on YouTube, I'm on my phone, on my X-box, on my Apple TV, whatever it is that I'm doing—I'm not going to leave to visit your website.

You have to make it very clear why you want them to leave. "Come here and I'm going to give you this," or "Come here and you're going to get that." Make it very clear why they need to do it now, as opposed to in the future. Give them a reason and you'll have a lot more chances for them to actually link to something outside of YouTube.

Finally, just speak to anything that might not show up on their page. You have annotations, you have a bunch of things. You should say in the video, "Look, if you're watching this on your computer, there are 47 ways to visit my website or find out other things that I'm doing. But of course if you're watching this on your phone, you don't have those options, so you might as well X." That makes complete sense, people enjoy it, people appreciate it. And that's how you get your videos to link outside of YouTube.

Summary

The reason YouTube makes it challenging to link videos to outside of its site is because of the potential dangers, such as links that send people to malware or spyware sites that would quickly damage YouTube's reputation and create a slew of problems. In this case, it's valuable to be a YouTube partner, where YouTube may allow you to link to an external site if they trust you.

However, there are several ways to link to external videos without this partner relationship:

- ❖ Ask people to go to the link within your video, by saying, "Please visit www.x.com."

- ❖ Add text within your video that asks people to go to www.x.com.

- ❖ Include http://www.x.com within the description of your video.

- ❖ Link to your Google+ page, and provide the external link there.

- ❖ Include the outside link in an annotation.

If you are concerned with driving traffic to an external link, remember that some people could be viewing on mobile devices and tailor accordingly. For example, including a message that sends people to an external link as text within your video is ideal because it presents no problems across problems.

Action Items

1. Try as many of the strategies listed as possible, to link outside of YouTube: include the link within your video, but also include it in your description.

2. Make it very clear where the link will bring them. For example, "To learn more about this topic, visit my website X."

3. Make it clear why your viewer should visit the link now as opposed to in the future.

4. Address all the different ways people can reach your external links, within your video. Be clear what the options are for people on desktop computers, and what the options are for people watching your video on their mobile device, etc.

QUESTION FIFTEEN

What Is The Best Format For A YouTube Video?

YouTube takes any format you send them, so don't worry about it. Do they take X? Yes. Do they take Y? Yes. Do they take Mac? Linux? Windows? Yes, yes, and yes.

YouTube will take any video format produced by any major, realistic video editing system. So don't worry about trans-coding or formatting for YouTube, just give them what you've got and let them take it from there. They will do everything they can to make it look as good as is possible.

Now realize, if you send them a dead duck, it's still a dead duck—it might be one of the best looking dead ducks they've ever had. Send them high quality, send them whatever format you want, and YouTube will make it look as good as possible.

It's part of what makes YouTube so cool: you don't have to worry about the format, bitrates, codecs and all these things you may have heard of or even worried about.

I did a production and event where we did all the promotion across YouTube and saw tens of thousands of views of YouTube over the course of a week. Looking at the statistics and analytics for our whole program, and we saw that there were hundreds of phone types that we didn't even know existed. (We could only find about half of them on the Internet with specs in English.) People come from all over the world, and the great thing was phones that I didn't know existed, with media players that I had never heard of, were consuming the content coming from YouTube.

That's the power of YouTube. Definitely leverage that.

The great thing is, because they'll take any format, you can just send it to them and then breathe a sigh of relief. Keep your focus on the content instead.

The action items are simple. Worry about the content, not the format, and send the best quality video that you can.

Summary

The Good News: Don't worry about the format of your video; YouTube will do everything they can to make it look as good as possible.

The fact is that YouTube will accept any format that you

send them: Mac, Linux, and Windows. Simply, don't worry about the format of your video. It is in YouTube's best interest to optimize all of the videos to make them look as attractive as possible on their website. This is a crucial factor in what makes YouTube such a ubiquitous and powerful tool: you never have to worry about codecs, bitrates, or audio formats.

More Good News: Your video will work on all technology.

Furthermore, you can trust that your videos will function on hundreds and hundreds (if not all) devices. People with technology from all over the world can still access YouTube and see your videos in fantastic picture quality. Understand YouTube's prowess in digital formatting, and take a deep sigh of relief.

Action Items

1. Don't worry about formatting.

2. Trust YouTube's ability to make your video function on all platforms.

QUESTION SIXTEEN

What Should I Do After I Publish My YouTube Video?

What should you do after you publish your YouTube video, to get the most views and traffic as possible? Fact number one is that YouTube weighs their rankings strongly based on how long people watch the video, and they've said this publicly time and time again.

Your strategy is to get as many people as possible who actually watch the video to the end, to watch the video.

Don't do anything silly like buy views or get a bunch of people to click on the video and then leave. If you get a couple hundred people to view the video four to five seconds into a four-minute video, you're directly telling YouTube that people aren't finding what it is that this video had promised. Subsequently, you get pushed into a ghetto of sorts—and you don't want that.

So realize that they weigh strongly on how long people watch the video, and never do anything silly like buying views or traffic.

What are your action items? How can you get high quality views?

Number one, when you publish a video, immediately send it to all the social media channels and audiences that you have access to, that are interested in the topic you made your video about.

This is important: some people may have friends from Church that they send their video about their sandwich store, and if the friends don't care—they may still click just to see what crazy Frank is up to—they are not going to watch the video through to the end. You should link to social media that relates to the topic of your video, and in that case you are going to get full views.

Twitter links to people interested in the topic that you have written about, the topic that you've done makes great sense, you get immediate clicks and immediate results. Embedding pages on Pinterest about your specific topic is also a great way to see some really, really cool results for your YouTube videos.

Google+ is good for a number reasons. You don't necessarily get a lot of humans looking at the Google+ pages, but you get Google+ and a bunch of other interesting areas.

If I go to my YouTube homepage, I'll see different friends who have shared content on Google+. These are all people that I'm following on Google+, who shared things and because they shared them on Google+, they showed up on my YouTube page. So yes, people that your audience follows on Google+, that they follow on YouTube, will still show up on their YouTube homepage.

Again, immediately send your video to all the social media that's interested in the video you made about X.

Number two, if you have a list about the topic X, you definitely want to email it the video link to them. If you don't have a list related to that topic X, and you're marketing on the Internet about topic X, build that list.

Now, there has been some training out there in the industry advising you to send members of your list to your blog. That's wrong. Send them straight to YouTube. It's friendly, it's where the nice kitty videos are, and it's where people go to access videos quickly and easily. Definitely send people directly to YouTube the second you go live.

Now once that is done, take the video and embed the video on your blog. This will trigger some people who follow your blog. Again, if you have an email list, send them straight to YouTube. The embedding on the blog is just a secondary alert to Google that you've got content about the topic elsewhere, that is by embedding the video, essentially giving it a thumbs up that it is about the content at hand.

Finally, encourage everybody to make comments, and do that inside of the video itself. Comments, thumbs up, shares, and embeds on other websites send social signals, and the domino effect that comes from that is quite tremendous. Make social part of your videos by encouraging people in annotations, to reach people watching on their computers, or within the content, for people watching on their phones.

All you have to do is say, "When you're done with this video give us thumbs up on your phone." Encourage people to make comments, integrate accordingly and you will do really well.

That's what you do immediately after publishing your YouTube video that gets you the most views and traffic from people who are likely to view it to the end. Accordingly, Google will see what you're doing, take you seriously and will then start sending more people to you based on the key words and the topic that you are about.

Summary

Remember, YouTube places a lot of emphasis on how long people spend watching your video. Accordingly, your strategy should be to find as many people as possible who are interested in your topic and will watch your video from beginning to end. Avoid any sort of purchased traffic or anybody that promises you thousands of hits; most likely it will be detrimental to your business. If people only spend a few seconds watching your five minute video, YouTube will conclude that your video is irrelevant and a poor search result for its keyword.

<u>The Bottom Line:</u> Focus on viewers who are interested in your topic.

Action Items

1. Publish new of your video to all social media platforms relevant to the topic of your video. Find pages with followers who are interested in your topic on Facebook, Twitter, Pinterest, and Google+.

2. Email your list about your new video, as long as subscribers to that list are interested in your topic. If you don't have a list related to the topic of your video, build one prior to launching your video.

3. Link people directly to the YouTube link, rather than sending them to a blog.

4. Embed your video in your blog. This acts a secondary alert to Google that your video is

relevant and on topic.

5. Encourage viewers to comment on and like your video. Do this within your video as a call to action or annotation, and when posting on your social media channels.

QUESTION SEVENTEEN

When Should I Use YouTube And The YouTube Player? When Should I Not?

This is a great question asked by numerous people. A lot of people say, "If you put up a video on YouTube, people can click over to YouTube, or can find related videos and people can do all sorts of things that they shouldn't do. Yes the YouTube player is easy but I don't want to do it for those reasons."

Let's review the facts. Number one, YouTube is extremely friendly, extremely safe, and their player is going to work on every machine, phone, and tablet. The fancy video player that you put on your website might not work on the very device that people are looking at. I've yet to see an international video player that one can buy that works with absolutely everything. Nothing is more frustrating than visiting a website that says "Click here to play," and have that not work.

Since YouTube is going to work on every machine, phone and tablet and you can put that on your website, and know the content is going to be consumed. You are not going to be producing frustration in your customer and audience base.

Realize that more often than not, that the positives of having the YouTube player are going to out weigh the negatives. Using a fancy video player that people don't know how to use, they might struggle just to find the play button. Realize your audience has done YouTube, so your audience knows YouTube. Integrating the YouTube player into your website is going to make the experience easy and familiar; it's going to be exactly what people want.

YouTube gives videos the strongest rankings that actually have people watching videos all the way through—that's the number one ranking. The best way to do that is to get them a video where they can see how long the video is going to be. You've got a video that matches on your site, it's comfortable, there are no questions. If people know exactly the experience they are going to get, then you have a better chance of them completing things accordingly.

People from your site are the ones most likely to watch your videos all the way to the end, because people from your site are the ones who like you the most. So putting a YouTube video and getting the power of showing YouTube to the people who watch this to the end, because it's people from your website, does incredibly well. So basically if at all possible, use the YouTube player.

You should not use the YouTube player when A, you're doing something extremely commercial that will get you banned from YouTube. Look up the community standards inside of YouTube, YouTube tells you what you can and cannot do. If you have a video that's going to break the rules on what it is that you can't do, then definitely don't do it! For goodness' sakes, don't get yourself banned. In light of all the work you did to get your video on YouTube, doing something silly and like this just doesn't make sense.

So use the third party video player there, but honestly, you still mght want to use one that looks like YouTube.

Finally there is a value call that the possibility of them leaving your site by clicking on the link inside the YouTube player outweighs the benefits of using the YouTube player. If the chance of them leaving is that big and that dangerous, (I really have found very few times and it actually is) then put up your own site. But when it comes down to it, nine times out of a 100 (if not more), using the YouTube video player on your site is going to make a lot more sense.

Once again, the action items are simple.

First, use the video player whenever you possibly can.

And secondly, realize you can check or uncheck the option to "Show suggested videos," so at least they will not be automatically promoting somebody else at the end. But do use the YouTube player whenever you can because the positives so often out weigh the negatives.

Summary

YouTube is extremely friendly, safe, and functions across machines and platforms. The reason YouTube is the best player to use, is because it guarantees that your content will be consumed flawlessly, and you will not produce any sort of tech-aggravation in your viewers. In most cases, the advantages of the YouTube player significantly outweigh the disadvantages.

If you do use a different player, you run into the problem of users who aren't accustomed to the technology. Any sort of road bump or bottleneck creates an opportunity to lose that viewer, and make your work less impactful. Everybody (more or less) knows how to use YouTube; that YouTube logo and video player design immediately signal to somebody that the video is in a familiar format, and it will be easy to view. Also, remember, that since Google gives the strongest rankings to videos that are watched all the way through, having a video that shows the total time at the bottom bar, as YouTube does, is a great advantage.

The Bottom Line: The YouTube Player is friendly,

familiar, and functional, and maximizes viewership.

There are only two scenarios in which you shouldn't use the YouTube Player: A) You are doing something incredibly commercial and your video doesn't comply with YouTube's rules and regulations (Check the community standards thoroughly to make sure you don't break any rules!). B) Your priority is keeping people on your site, and the danger of them clicking on other links within the YouTube Player and clicking away from your site is greater than the benefit of using the YouTube Player.

Action Items

1. Use the YouTube Video Player when you can.

2. Don't use the YouTube Video Player if you're not complying with their rules.

3. Embed videos in a way that prevents other videos from being advertised at the end of your video, if you feel it is necessary.

QUESTION EIGHTEEN

Is It Better To Have One YouTube Channel For Everything I Do?

This is a question that I get asked all the time, and it's a great strategy question that absolutely makes sense. Is it better to have one YouTube channel for everything or one YouTube channel for every niche you happen to find yourself involved with? Let's walk through the intelligence here.

YouTube accounts are free. It's not that difficult to sign up for a different account or channel because they are free, and the option is always there. YouTube used to put a lot of weight on how much action and how many videos your channel had.

We now know that YouTube puts more weight on how long the videos are viewed. Therefore, the benefit of having a channel with a lot of views isn't as strong as it used to be. If you're looking to the future and tracking where things are going, you are going to find considerably more that type of focus.

In fact, the old partner program seems to have disappeared. Aren't I a partner? There is a new program, where if you place an ad on any of your YouTube videos, you are a partner. However, most of the reasons for having a YouTube channel with a lot of videos and a lot of subscribers have gone away.

All in all, this speaks to having different channels for different niches.

Remember that you can cross promote channels. If you have five channels, each of the five channels can promote back to one channel, and you can create a network. There are certainly some internal ranking features that exist there.

Also, keep in mind that it is considerably easier to promote people to a certain channel about a certain topic. For example, I do send people to my YouTube Channel "Colligan"—something that I created a long time ago that has too many views to let go of. But think about it, what is "Colligan" about?

Now, I also have a YouTube channel called "Paul's iPad." That one is easy: it's about iPads. Making a channel specific to what you've got will let people know exactly what's there, and won't waste people's time. If you're matching your videos to an audience, they will watch them to the end—it makes sense.

However, bear in mind that people can get very easily distracted when they are managing a myriad of channels. I've seen people who have spent 80 percent of their week managing all their YouTube channels, and only 20 percent making content. For goodness' sake, spend your time on content and don't worry about these things.

Is it better to have one channel for everything or one per niche? I would say one per niche, unless that's going to be a distraction for you—and that's something only you can answer.

Let's review your action items for this question.

One channel per niche or topic is great. Just don't spend a lot of time administrating or managing your channels.

Also, I do strongly suggest that you sit down and consider how many topics and niches you should be involved with at any given time. Twenty channels with one video in each channel is not going to do that well for you, whereas if you put those 20 videos about a given niche on one channel, you may do much better.

In conclusion, do consider creating one channel per niche, but be strategic about it.

Summary

One great feature of YouTube is that creating new

channels and uploading content is unlimited, so there is no end to the number of unique channels you can create. Furthermore, with a shift in emphasis on the length of video watched, the number of channel views have become less of a priority. Many of the benefits of having a lot of subscribers to your channel, like gaining partner status, have diminished. In conclusion, it does make sense to have a different channel that speaks to particular niches.

The Bottom Line: There is no particular benefit to having all of your views and visits on one channel.

Remember that you can also cross promote channels, and that it's significantly easier to promote a channel with a clear, explicit topic. Somebody interested in iPads is much more likely to go to "Paul's iPad Channel" than they are to go to "Colligan Channel." Let people know upfront what your channel is about, and people will be grateful that you didn't waste their time.

Are there any drawbacks? Yes, of course there are. Don't get too carried away creating too many channels. You don't want to end up spending 80% of your time managing channels, and only 20% of your time creating new content. So the task is to create as many channels as you can handle without getting too distracted.

The Common Pitfall: Don't create so many channels that you spend all your time managing them.

Action Items

1. Create one channel per niche or topic.

2. Beware of spending too much time administering your channels—only create as many as you can manage.

3. Create enough content for each channel. Don't end up with 20 channels with only one video on each channel.

QUESTION NINETEEN

When Should I Let YouTube Place Ads On My Videos?

"YouTube asks about placing ads on my videos. YouTube talks about partnering with me. When should I let YouTube place ads on my videos?"

Well the first thing I want to point out, and this is just a simple fact, the money from advertising YouTube videos is downright silly. There is no other way to put it. It's just not viable.

For example, I've put ads on videos that have had over a million views across my channels, and I've collected...$200 cash. I haven't put commercials across to all my videos by any means, but still, the number is pretty low. It's around the tune of $2 to $5 per 1,000 views—which is almost laughable.

So letting YouTube place ads on your videos just for the cash doesn't make sense unless you go viral or you're just the type of person who has millions of people viewing your videos. If you can pull that off—great. But in reality, that's just a lot more work and a lot more effort than a lot of people make it out to be.

There is a strategy to letting YouTube put ads on your videos that you really want to think about. Fact one, when Google has no sponsored video for your term, they might actually put up your video as a sponsored video if it has an ad on it. Why? Because that ad makes them money.

Think about it, let's imagine your term is "Glass Houses", and they don't have sponsored videos for glass houses. Consequently, you have a video about glass houses that has an ad on it. Guess what? YouTube makes money if your video shows up in sponsored results. I have seen that happen, and I have seen thousands of views come by placing ads on specific videos.

Honestly, I have yet to see an ad that distracts my audience. Though I've never seen a competitor's ad in any of my videos, that is possible, and you might want to monitor the ads for quality assurance. But I have seen thousands of views brought in by YouTube as a result of this strategy, so keep it in mind.

Again, realize that YouTube makes money from the ads. Accordingly, YouTube looks at all the partners and says, "Which of the partners have I made money from? Which of the channels have I made money from?" Those are the ones that they are going to promote the most. So if you include ads on a couple of videos, you are going to do better on your YouTube channel than people who don't.

What are your action items related to letting YouTube place ads on your videos?

Number one, regardless of what you do, throw ads on one or two videos. The protection that comes from doing so is never bad thing: YouTube sees you as a player, as a member of the team, and that video will be viewed every once in a while. (In fact, I've known people who have put up videos for the specific purpose of housing ads, to distract YouTube from the content that they don't put ads on.)

Finally, check your video for the terms that you're about to produce a video for, and see if there are any other sponsored ads that come up. If there are, and they're exactly on your topic, you might not want to play this game at all.

If there aren't any sponsored videos on your keywords or topic, it means that if you put an ad on that video, you could become a sponsored video, and get more clicks. It's a great way to get you to the top of the list without special optimization efforts, and it kills two birds with one stone.

Let YouTube place ads on your videos—it's advantageous

to you. Think a big picture, think long term and you can and will do quite well.

Summary

Before you think about allowing YouTube to place ads in your videos, understand that the amount of money you can make is marginal. The profits are in the neighborhood of $2-$5 per 1,000 views. In short, if you do utilize ads, don't do it for the cash.

However, there are two compelling reasons to incorporate ads into your videos or channel:

- ❖ Being a sponsored video on Google. If Google doesn't have a sponsored video for your particular keyword or topic, but your video has an advertisement in it, your video may become featured just by virtue of the advertising. Therefore, allowing YouTube to advertise with you may result in more hits.

- ❖ Being promoted within YouTube. YouTube wants to make money from their advertisements. If they see that they make more money from some partners than others, they are more likely to promote high profit partners; it's that simple.

Action Items

1. Allow ads on one or two of your videos. YouTube will value you as a player and a partner, and you will get preferential treatment within the search engine.

2. Search to see if there are any other videos that show up for your keywords in the sponsored video bar of Google before deciding which videos to partner with advertising. Choose words that aren't being sponsored, giving your video a chance to appear in the coveted spot.

QUESTION TWENTY

What Are The Best Third Party Tools And Services For YouTube?

You may have searched the Internet, seen videos, or read articles claiming that there are third party tools and services that you can use with YouTube that will do well for you.

What should you do? What should your strategy be?

Number one, this is incredibly important, (at least at the time of publication of this book) YouTube terms and services say specifically that you cannot use any software that accesses their servers faster than a human can in the same amount of time. They are not against robots, mechanics, or automation, but they are against automation mechanics that acts faster than a human.

Those are YouTube's rules—and it's something that you can debate until the end of time if you wish—but you have agreed to play by them. YouTube doesn't want your tools to go faster than a human can, so quite simply, don't use anything that goes faster than a human can.

Number two, YouTube has an API for people that don't want to admit they are a machine. YouTube is fine with machines and software, but you definitely want to use their special API, because you don't want to pretend to be anything other than what you really are.

If you pretend on any element of your website or your videos, YouTube will start to think, "Is this person not real in some other element? Is there something else we need to worry about?" You don't want any question marks associated with your account; be transparent.

Based on my experience—and I'm not a lawyer, don't play one on TV—anybody who follows the rules of YouTube's Terms of Service and uses the API for third party software doesn't experience any problems.

However, if you use a tool with the API to get a bunch of videos that are viewed for five seconds, that will only result in a low quality score, and could bring you more damage than good. You might get 1,000 views, but if your video never comes up in search results for those 1,000 views, does it really matter?

Most importantly, match the right audiences to your videos, ones that will actually be interested in viewing your content. Don't just try to bump up your numbers to make mom feel proud of that click count. Using third party tools and services is one method, but it's not the only way.

As YouTube gets more and more mature, third party tools are becoming less and less viable as a core strategy. Make this far down on your list, it certainly shouldn't be at the top. Once you have kind of mastered everything else, find the tool that plays by the rules, uses the API and go from there.

What are the action items?

If there is a significant audience online that is your exact demographic, the mechanization of a third party might be strategic for you. At that point, explore the tools, but be sure they utilize the API, that you never pretend to be anything other than who you are, and that you follow YouTube's and Google's Terms and Services.

In short, my Mom always said, *"If it seems too good to be true, it probably is."* That's the case: if you find a tool or service that promises the world, I would be skeptical.

At the time of this writing, there are only two tools that I can recommend that utilize the API, follow the Terms and Services, and produce nice results.

One of them is Traffic Geyser, a video submission service that—in full disclosure—I work for. *Make of that disclosure what you will ;-) If you register your book (as per the option at the front), I'll get you free access to the tool to try it out.*

Tube Tool Book is another great tool that I have used in the past to great success, and haven't encountered any problems with thus far.

Today, I can recommend those two services now, and there may be others that I'm unaware of, but realize that these things are constantly changing.

Follow the terms and conditions, make use of the API, be strategic about it and you'll do well with third party services.

Again, in this crazy YouTube world, these things can change at any time.

Summary

Most likely you've seen or read about third party tools and services that you can use to boost your video's or channel's effectiveness. Keep in mind that YouTube does not permit any software that accesses their servers faster than human beings. So, in order to comply with their rules, don't employ a third party service that automates faster than humans can keep up with. Since YouTube doesn't have qualms with machines, they do have a special API for machines. Never try to hide anything from YouTube, or trick YouTube, because one question mark or moment of mistrust can ruin your relationship and spoil potential partnerships.

<u>The Common Pitfall:</u> Don't ever try to trick YouTube; be completely transparent.

Remember, even if you use a third party service, the ultimate goal is have people view your entire video, not to reach a hollow but high view count. Your priority is to find the right audience for your video. Stay away from services that create views shorter than five seconds, and make sure you follow the terms and services.

Action Items

1. Only use tools and services that target your key demographic, and not just short-lived views.

2. Utilize the API and be transparent with YouTube if you do use a third party tool.

3. Choose the right tool. Currently, I recommend Traffic Geyser and Tube ToolBox to help you get the right views and still comply with Terms and Conditions.

QUESTION TWENTY-ONE

Should I Use Services To Get More Views For My YouTube Videos?

You may have seen those sites where you can pay a few bucks and get tens of thousands of views. The burning question is, should you use those? Let's review the facts.

Google and YouTube are strongly ranking your video based on how long people actually watch it. This has two massive implications:

Number one, you don't want to make a video any longer than it should be, because if people don't watch to the end, Google is not going to rank you as well as you would like them to.

Number two, you want to make sure that people watch to the end, which means you want a market to message match for the people who are actually consuming the video. Realize who your audience is, and only have your audience watch the videos. Then, realize what your audience needs and give them videos that give them that, and absolutely nothing else.

What does this have to do with the buying of views?

The really cool implication of YouTube's new ranking system, is that a video with a focused audience can do battle with a video that has million of views. Use this to your advantage.

Now, most of the services that promise the too good to be true stuff, A, cheat, and B, use two to five seconds of a video at the most. They view enough to get that count click but they don't view enough to get the quality click that you're looking for. Even if you get 10 or 20 seconds of viewership, you're going to look really bad because people aren't watching to the end.

In short, know that these services do this to get the viewer count up, but aren't concerned view quality. You could buy 10,000, 20,000 views and do tremendous amounts of damage to your ranking because YouTube cares only about how long people watch. The answer is that you should not use these services to get more views for your videos 99.99 percent of the time.

Now there are some interesting programs out there, such as Virool. What's interesting about this tool is that it's essentially a pay-per-view mechanism, one that is realistic and not based in robots that are hitting the refresh button all the time. Similar to Ads.YouTube.com, if you're paying to match the audience with the message, you're at an interesting place.

Your action items for this question are simple.

Ask yourself if this is the best strategy. Considering the new Google algorithm and the new YouTube management system, buying high quality views is going to get expensive. You're going to work really hard to get about three cents per view. Really, you are going to be looking at about eight to ten cents per view, which gets really expensive.

Also, you have to ask why you're trying to get those additional views. If you're trying to get the additional views to impress other people when they come in, you have to take into account that buying 10,000 views will bring you to the bottom of the search. Is that worth it? The answer is no, and YouTube is tracking you all the time, searching for cheaters.

If you have a valid reason to buy views, buy them strategically. But realize with the new situation inside of YouTube, the reasons to buy views are diminishing, so select your strategy accordingly.

Summary

You may have seen services that promise thousands of views to your videos in exchange for a small sum. Again,

Google and YouTube rank your videos based on how long people watch the videos—not how many clicks they receive. Using a service that gets you views, but not watches, means that Google will notice your videos are being prematurely terminated and will conclude that they are irrelevant to those keywords. You only want your target audience to be watching your videos. Understand what people need to see or hear, and create it for them.

<u>The Good News:</u> Good content is rewarded, and (most) purchased traffic is not.

What's the implication of Google and YouTube's new ranking system? This means that a high quality video that received its views by virtue of the value of its content can compete with videos that purchased clicks. Many of the services make promises that aren't feasible, and most likely get you views by cheating, only focusing on clicks and not viewership.

<u>The Bottom Line:</u> Do not use services that promise views on YouTube. Your priority is getting people to watch your videos to the end.

Alternatively, there are tools that operate on a pay-per-view model, such as Virool. You can also utilize Ads.YouTube.com, and pay to receive views from an audience that actually wants to hear your message.

Action Items

1. Be strategic: will using services that promise views really pay off?

2. Ask yourself why you are trying to get those additional views: is it just for the number next to the video? Make quality and not quantity your priority.

3. Don't purchase services unless they can give you full views from audience members who are interested in your content.

Now What?

Now What?

As I mentioned at the beginning of this book, YouTube will change. If you register this book (either by visiting:

http://0s4.com/r/YTSB

Or scanning this QR code:

I'll make sure to keep you up to date with the latest, and send you access to more than 3 hours of additional YouTube training – including a 75 minute training on how to make the most of the new YouTube OneChannel format.

If you have any questions about what's in this book, you

can grab me on one of the social networks or, better yet, you can ask a question on my page at Amazon. I'm sure not going to leave any question open for too long:

http://www.PaulColligan.com/Amazon

I'd also recommend that you subscribe to my channel at YouTube.

http://www.youtube.com/subscription_center?add_user=colligan

Want 21 (free) videos about YouTube and marketing on YouTube? Take a look at -

http://www.21QuestionsAboutYouTube.com

If you'd like to register your book so I can keep you up to date when we make changes (and, with YouTube, you know it will be often), take a look at –

http://www.YouTubeStrategiesBook.com

As I mentioned at the beginning of this book, I'll update this (for those who registered their book through one of these two choices) when the need arises. I'll do the forced Kindle Update thing whenever I can but, if you want to follow me on one of the social networks, you'll know the instant I change things.

Here are those links again:

http://PaulColligan.com/YouTube
http://PaulColligan.com/GooglePlus
http://PaulColligan.com/Amazon
http://PaulColligan.com/Twitter
http://PaulColligan.com/Facebook
http://YouTubeStrategiesBook.com